GIRLS WHO AIN'T AFRAID TO CURSE WHEN COMMUNICATING WITH GOD

A 31-DAY SELF-STUDY GUIDE TO SPIRITUAL LIBERATION

SO
FUNDAMENTAL

Girls Who Ain't Afraid to Curse When Communicating With God: A 31-Day Self-Study Guide to Spiritual Liberation

Published by: So Fundamental Publications™

Printed in the United States of America

ISBN: 0-9886251-8-0

ISBN-13: 978-0-9886251-8-1

Special discounts are available on bulk quantity purchases by book clubs, associations and special interest groups. For details email: Trelani@SoFundamental.com

For more information, log onto

www.GirlsWhoAintAfraid.com

Co-edited by Trelani Michelle and Jayla Lawton

DEDICATION

This book is dedicated to the girl who never felt like she was enough

The girl who wears bright pink lipstick even though society tells her she's too dark

The girl who tries her best to accept what she sees in the mirror

The girl at war with her own mind

Feels like she doesn't truly fit in anywhere

Picking up her pieces after a heartbreak

Wanting desperately to be seen, heard, and understood

Ready but afraid to finally share her same-gender love to those who love her

Might be depressed but instead feels like she's failing

Has dissociated herself from her body

Prefers pants over skirts or skirts over pants

Feels like her house is more of a hell than a home

Uses jokes to mask her pain

Uses sex to cope

Unsure what she wants for lunch, let alone what she wants to do for the rest of her life

Learning when to say no and when to say yes

Finds self-care in material things and solitude

Intent on being her best self despite physical health challenges

Been burned by her girl friends

On her second, third, or fourth strike

Wondering if she needs professional help

No longer afraid to get help

On a hell of a journey to forgive herself

Needs to know that she has the right to change her mind about whatever, whenever

Ready to accept and express her most authentic self

This book is dedicated to the girl who ain't afraid to curse when communicating with God

CONTENTS

HOW TO USE THIS GUIDE

This book contains thirty-one self-guiding studies, each consisting of a Spirit quote, warm-up prompt, introspective lesson, and suggested meditation. Prompts and meditations consist of exercises like visualization, journaling, breathing exercises, dancing, chanting, mirror work, and more to facilitate self-inquiry, intention-setting, emotional release, and chakra balancing.

You will need the following:

- a space where you feel comfortable doing the above-mentioned activities;

- a pen and notebook;

- a calendar;

- a mirror;

- a timer; and

- at least thirty minutes to complete each study.

The prompts are designed to get you in the groove for the study and to initiate self-exploration. Most of them call for writing. Though we have digital options, your writing allows for far more spiritual access and fewer distractions. The activity from the prompt leads you directly into the lesson, which is meant to give you the *why* behind the work. Afterward, we flow right into either a resting or active meditation.

Begin resting meditations by sitting or lying comfortably and relaxing your eyes, which you may want to open or close, depending on personal comfort. Engage in deep breathing to calm your thoughts and settle your awareness. During meditation, we may use a mantra, which is a repeated sound, word, or statement; a visualization, which is using your imagination; or a simple focus on the flow of your breathing. If you're new to meditation, aim for ten-minute sessions. If you're more seasoned, make twenty minutes your minimum. Timers help a lot.

Following this guide from front to back ain't necessary. Flip to a random page or browse the table of contents for a lesson you feel fits in that particular moment. This is your experience.

Also, we're not trying to get you to go to church, read the bible, or stop going/reading. Do you. We're just encouraging you to deepen your relationship with whatever you believe. Make sure you're committed to it because it works for you, not because you grew up doing it. Be intentional about that thang; that's all we're saying.

Our book's (amazing) copyeditor, Karen Leonard, summarized her personal experience in a way that articulates exactly what we mean. She said, "One of the reasons I'm becoming Jewish is because they're far more comfortable cursing, questioning, and arguing with God than a lot of Christian denominations. In fact, the word 'Israel,' which refers to the Jewish people for Jews, means 'wrestles with God.' It reminds me of an inscription on the wall in a concentration camp that says, 'If there is a God, he'll have to beg me for forgiveness.' That quote has always stuck with me, and, even though I've never suffered anything close to that, I feel it."

She's choosing to become Jewish *intentionally*. That's all we're saying here. Choose what works for you, whether that happens to be what was passed down to you or not. Make sure there's room in your belief for who you are, as well as room to grow. Make sure you feel comfortable and confident in your communication with whomever or whatever you deem to be the highest power.

On a final note, this book is not intended or implied to be a substitute for professional medical advice, diagnosis, or treatment. Never disregard professional medical advice or delay seeking medical treatment because of something you read in this book.

Cool? Cool.

HEY!

The imaginary God my grandmother and Sunday school taught me as a child made absolutely no sense. He was a walking-dead contradiction. I didn't understand the Holy Trinity, either, the belief in the Son, a Father, and Holy Spirit. The Son and the Father were above humanity, yet given human qualities. What did that mean? I couldn't picture them. Spirit, I could. Spirit showed up and showed out every Sunday at church when one of the members broke out into a shout and raced down the aisle. But God? His heaven didn't excite me, but his hell scared the shit out of me, so I fumbled along anyhow. The older I got, the more I felt like I was already living in hell. Being accustomed to it, my fear of eternal burning dissipated.

By the time I was twelve, I quit praying. I was tired of how unattached, repetitive, and inauthentic it felt. I craved a different perspective and was curious how others lived. I started hanging out with people who didn't go to church and started watching shows that came on way after my bedtime. I preferred this way of life to religion. Being religious was like having more parents with far more rules governing what I could and couldn't do. I couldn't wait to be free, to have somewhere else to lay my head.

Unable to be or feel free, journaling was my best solution. It's where I carried my curiosities, completed my thoughts, wrote my poetry, started my fiction, and dreamed about a life that was worlds away from the run-of-the-mill, no-soul-having one I was living.

One night, a monsoon of grief washed over me. My romantic relationship was in off mode, bank account was in the negative, job wasn't at all secure, baby was colicky, and I was missing my grandmother. I decided to journal and found myself writing a letter to God. I felt hopeless and needed to give him a piece of my mothafucking mind. (It still makes the hairs on my arms stand up to say that.) The moment was so intense that, afterward, I fell into the deepest sleep I've ever had. After a conversation like that, I couldn't go back to a fake-ass, god-fearing existence. Something had stirred inside of me. It's like my ancestors started nodding like, "Yep, she's ready."

When I broke down that night, although I had confronted the man who demanded that the *g* in his name be capitalized, it was Spirit who comforted me—Spirit, who had moved me as a child in church, who I felt we were all praying to and worshipping, a maternal presence, a force that shows up uniquely for every being. In my confrontation, Spirit didn't mind my anger or even my cursing because I surely didn't soften what I really wanted to say. I spoke what was on my heart in the exact way that it showed up for me and I felt celebrated for it. That's when my real relationship with Spirit started, and through her, my relationship with God. Until about a month ago, I had never shared that facet of my spirituality with anyone—let alone on social media—but one day I decided to post this on Instagram:

I be wanting to speak on stuff sometimes, but Spirit be like, "Leave that shit alone, hear?" And I be like, "Yes, ma'am."

Posting that to the world was like rubbernecking before jumping into Double Dutch ropes. I had no clue how it would be accepted once I hit send. I remember changing the wording around and taking out the word "shit," but then I decided to keep it the way Spirit had given it to me. I reminded myself that our uninhabited selves, our authentic voices, and the way we speak when we're amongst our tribe are what reach the core of a person. That's what I'm in the business of doing.

So I posted it. And it was received well. So well that someone else screenshotted it, cropped my name out, and reposted it as if it were hers. She got thousands of likes for it and tons of comments to go with it. Was I offended? Hell yes! But it's one of those things that doesn't make sense to give energy to, so I consciously chose to embrace the fact that my truth had resonated with so many souls. That sat much better.

Then Akilah S Richards, my spiritual mentor/sister-friend, shared it with her circles. They loved it just as strongly. Akilah experiences Spirit in the way I do and texted me that I needed to be louder. I woke up the next morning to her invitation to a shared online document where she had created a thirty-one-day outline based on both of our Instagram posts. She explained, "When I was in the space of your word-flow, many of my own Spirit-be-like moments came to me, too." She asked if fleshing it out with prompts, expanded lessons, and suggested meditations was something that I'd be interested in.

I was. In 2016, I turned that outline into a book titled *Women Who Ain't Afraid to Curse When Communicating with God.* In 2019, I was invited to lead a workshop with A Revolutionary Summer, an all-girls summer camp in Baltimore. They had read *Women Who Ain't Afraid* and asked some really good questions about it. I'd already been considering writing a version for girls, and that workshop sealed it for me. I had to make it happen.

I didn't want to do it alone, though. Between mothering, teaching, and facilitating workshops, I know the wisdom that comes from the mouths of youth. I needed the girls to be an integral part of the book. In addition to their words being in the book, I wanted a girl to help me put it all together. There was only one girl I was interested in making that happen with.

Jayla.

I met her while teaching for a nonprofit in Savannah called The Deep Center. I connected with her instantly. I don't know what it was—it had it to be Spirit—but I loved her immediately. And we grew closer over the years. When she agreed to co-edit this book with me, I was incredibly excited and grateful.

Tight hugs,

Trelani

LESSON 1

Intention Setting: Intuition vs. Suppressors

I be wanting to speak on stuff sometimes but Spirit be like, "Leave that shit alone, hear?" And I be like, "Yes, ma'am." - Spirit speaking through Trelani Michelle (age 32 :: city 504)

Prompt: Make a list of instances in which you tend to react too quickly. Consider if and when you regret your verbal and physical actions, or lack thereof.

Story: Intuition is our internal GPS. It tells us when, where, and how to act, and with whom. For me, as a child, this voice sounded like my mama's, clear and booming. I knew when someone didn't have my best interest before they hurt me. If I ever felt like I wasn't safe, for whatever reason, my intuition turned my stomach and welled my eyes with tears.

Intuition can have suppressors though. For example, as children we were taught manners, requiring us to hug and kiss people with whom we don't want to share affection, like that auntie who always smacked her lips on our cheeks or that uncle who insisted we sit on his lap.

Suppressors force us to push down our natural desires and keep us from clearly knowing what's in our best interest. Suppressors can also make you feel safer in oppressive situations like schools that don't give a damn about your individuality, religions that make you feel powerless, relationships that make you feel not good enough, etc.

The good news is, as long as there is still breath in your body, your intuitive self is still present. She's still speaking. In fact, she never stopped. You just stopped listening. Come back home and reunite with the carefree, always-knowing little girl inside of you by listening to her and taking heed to what she tells you.

Meditation: Find a quiet space, clear of clutter. Get comfortable and begin taking long, deep breaths. Once relaxed, ask yourself what you want. Your answer is your intention. Once you've set your intention, relax your eyes. Listen. Your womb will tell you which thoughts are intuition and which are distractions. Just listen. Afterward, go back to the list you created in your prompt, and journal ways to integrate more of this intention into that list.

LESSON 2

When Home Feels Like Hell

"Your home is not four walls or the people within, and it's not your nightmares or doors slamming or people shouting. Your home is built the moment you look around and see the people closest to you loving you with unabashed joy." - Spirit speaking through Raya Tuffaha (age 20 :: city 206)

Prompt: Make a list of everyone who makes you feel good to be you, and then scribble something they did or said to make you feel that way.

Story: Like most kids, I sought my parents' approval—particularly my father's. After some time, I started to denounce my own aspirations and goals without even knowing it, and I centered my focus on fulfilling his vision to be the "perfect" child. Over time, I became more reserved than usual, numbed myself to stress-induced headaches, and took life more seriously than a non-taxpayer should. I had forgotten how to be a kid.

It took over ten years, but my awakening came in the form of a conversation. I had finally spoken to a relative (other than my mom) about the weight of the situation I was in. It took her, my aunt, to tell me it was not normal for a parent to constantly degrade his children when things didn't go his way, and that this was a sign of immaturity. For the first time, I had to look at my father as a human being instead of who I'd known him to be. Although the details of his past remain an enigma to

10

me, the ground on which we stand was enough to demand respect as his daughter and a fellow human. I had finally made my stand.

It's been over four years since I lived under his roof, and I miss it at times, but I do not regret choosing the route of healing over psychological bondage. Hopefully, he, too, will come to this realization. Somehow. Someday.

Meditation: Sit or lie comfortably. Relax your whole body. Keeping your eyes closed, think of someone who loves you (from the past or the present). Imagine them standing on your right side, sending you their love and wishing for your safety, well-being, and happiness. Feel that warmth from them to you. Now imagine the same person or another person who loves you deeply. Picture that person standing on your left side, wishing you safety, wellness, and happiness. Feel the kindness and warmth from them to you. Now imagine you're surrounded on all sides by everyone who loves you and has loved you. Bask in their prayers and love for you coming from all sides.

LESSON 3

Finding the Light

"You never completely discover yourself. Instead, you undergo a daily ritual of refining what already existed and remembering what they teach us to forget: we have always been light. Revolving, evolving, in a constant state of radiation." - Spirit speaking through Sierra Vincent (age 20 :: city 912)

Prompt: At the top of your paper, write "I am light." Set a timer for seven minutes and write whatever comes to mind next. Keep going. Don't stop writing, even if you're just repeating.

Story: A meditation practice called "yoga nidra" explains that we have five bodies/koshas. The first is your physical body. The second is the energy body, which works with the breath. The third is the mental/emotional. That's where we tend to spend the most time: in our mind and in our feelings. We're constantly thinking, reacting, wanting, and feeling. The fourth is the wisdom body, which is where your intuition lives. The fifth is called the "bliss body," which is our real self, who we are at your core: in other words, pure consciousness. It's who you were before you discovered hurt—your actual, undisturbed, most authentic self. The closest thing to God.

We developed a personality, a mask, to get through this thing called life. To survive. It happens around eight years old. As our environments change, so does our personality. Growing up in an abusive household affects your personality differently from someone who grows up in a safe household. Our mental/emotional body also defines "beautiful" and "cool" (which it got from the media and the opinions of those around us), and we compare ourselves to that.

It's important to check in with yourself. Who got you not liking yourself and your stuff? Why don't you like your stomach, your neighborhood, your family, your softness, your dominance? Is it a necessary dislike? Sometimes it is (i.e., I'm rude, and it's a reason I'm this way, but it ain't necessary no more). A lot of times it's an unnecessary dislike. Check in to see. And if you choose to change, be compassionate with yourself through the process.

Like Poetic.arreis, one of this book's contributors, said, "Aren't vulnerable and naked one and the same? But we love one and run from the other. I found love between three rolls of boy shorts and a 14" x 48" mirror. I got married in front of that mirror. For better or for worse ... for stretch marks, for dark marks, this matrimony wasn't gonna tarnish, because it depended on so much more than me."

Meditation: If you have access to a camera (camera phone is perfect), record your face for three minutes. It might feel awkward, but stick with it. Afterward, go back and play it. Look in your eyes. Is sadness there? Joy? Uncertainty? Does the mood change? No judgement here; it's just a check-in. We can fool ourselves sometimes, but our eyes don't lie.

LESSON 4

Making the Decision to Live for Me

"At the end of the day, week, month, moment we have to live with ourselves, and I've learned that the decisions I'm most proud of are the ones made with my well-being in mind." - Spirit speaking through Mariah George (age 18 :: city 912)

> **Prompt:** Make a list of three decisions you made that you're not proud of. Then make a list of three decisions you made that you are proud of. What was the motivation behind each decision? Why did you (really) do it? Write that down too.

Story: I made a lot of wild decisions, many of which I ain't proud of. I carried that regret for a long time, and then I dropped it. Shame didn't look good on me. Shame leads you to lie or otherwise omit the truth. It separates you from love. It's hard to really get close to people, because you don't want your skeletons falling all over the place. So you only open yourself up a little bit. I loved hard, but I don't think I was allowing myself to be loved as hard.

My grandmother used to say, "If you don't want other people finding out about it, then you ain't got no business doing it." When I dropped the shame, I started living by this principle. And like Mariah said best, "The decisions that I'm most proud of are the ones I made with me in mind, my own well-being and peace of mind."

14

It didn't feel good hanging on to a friendship with someone who criticized everything about me, just because we'd been friends for over a decade. It didn't feel good going to bed every night wondering if I was shorting myself with the relationship I was in. It didn't feel good waking up stupid early for a job I was damn good at but not at all interested in. It didn't feel good sending my kids to a school that didn't honor who they were as individuals and creatives.

At different points in my life, I quit all that shit. And my wellbeing skyrocketed, and I'm definitely most proud of those decisions.

Meditation: Refer back to your writing prompt. Does it have anything in common with the motivation behind the decisions you *are* proud of? Mine had in common wanting to be free and to be happy. What's yours? Make it an "I deserve" statement; in other words, "I deserve to be happy and free." Now set a timer for three minutes and repeat your "I deserve" statement to yourself until the alarm sounds.

LESSON 5

My Grades Don't Define Me

"I never really gave a fuck about school, let alone grades, so bad grades don't mean shit to nobody but my parents. I knew I had enough talent that would overshadow any A, B, or C I had." - Spirit speaking through **Honey** (age 18 :: city 313)

Prompt: What things in your life make you feel smart, talented, and special? Make a list. It can be people, hobbies, jobs, conversations, anything. Try to list at least ten things.

Story: One of the hardest moments as a mama was watching my son fail in school. He didn't perform well, for a bunch of reasons. Mainly, his learning style didn't match their teaching style. Also, he just wasn't interested in what was being taught. At all. Between the disconnection and the disinterest, his grades lived at rock bottom. He was incredibly talented though, had mind-blowing questions, and had "old soul" answers to questions asked to him. I knew, however, that it was only a matter of time before school had him feeling stupid. So I pulled him out and homeschooled him. Then he moved with his dad (his choice), and now he's back in school. And the same issues are surfacing. And grades are a big deal in that house.

In a song called *Deep Reverence*, Big Sean says, "In high school I learned chemistry, biology. But not how to cope with anxiety or how I could feel like I'm by myself on an island with depression on all sides

16

of me." But that's capitalism. It's only interested in production. We have to take care of ourselves—as individuals and as tribes. So I remind my children often, my friends too, that none of that shit matters at the end of the day. Life has so many options on the table. If the option you want requires school success, there are plenty resources to help get you there. Then again, there are so many paths that could care less about letters on a piece of a paper.

Focus on your joy, baby. On your peace of mind. On what brings you closer to yourself. On what feels like ... yes! And have the courage to pursue it. The rest of that shit will work itself out. Trust me.

Meditation: Inhale. Now slowly lift your arms up to the sky. Imagine a bright yellow ball of light igniting in the center of your abdomen. As you exhale, lower your arms and say, "My power comes from within." Continue this up and down motion. Every time you inhale and lift your arms, imagine the ball of yellow light growing bigger and more vibrant. When the light has radiated throughout your body, bring your hands to your heart and thank Spirit for blessing you at birth with everything you need to accomplish what you want and need to do.

LESSON 6

What Happens When We Compare

"People don't really know theyselves, and they only know what other people tell them about theyselves. Like, it can be good or bad, and you don't really know what you actually like about yourself—what you actually want to fix about yourself—until somebody else tells you to."- Spirit speaking through Imani (age 13 :: city 912)

> **Prompt:** Make a list of the five people you spend the most time with. Now describe each of them with five adjectives (e.g., Kobe is kind, hilarious, blunt, honest, and gentle; Rente is assertive, confident, hilarious, decisive, and loyal).

Story: Without other people, we have nothing to weigh ourselves against. If you've never experienced hurt, you wouldn't be able to recognize happiness. If you've only lived in the light, you don't know what darkness is. Our relationships with other people show us to ourselves. We're mirrors for each other. The people around you teach you so much about yourself—directly and indirectly.

Directly, they might tell you that you're gorgeous, you're brilliant, you're a great friend, or maybe even that you're ugly. What do you do with that information though? What if you're told that when you're very young? What if you're told that repeatedly? At what point does it ingrain itself in you as the truth? In pre-K, a classmate told my daughter that her afro was ugly, and she has refused to wear her hair out ever since. Even though everyone else told her that her hair was beautiful, that one criticism stuck.

Jayla said once that a friend told her she was self-deprecating. In that moment, she got defensive. That hurts! Later on, though, she realized there was a lot of truth to it. Depression is normal. Our emotions are like waves; they have their highs and lows. In our grief, we can sometimes become cynical, pessimistic, and, yes, even self-deprecating. And without that honest person to check you, and the courage to ask yourself if there might be some truth in it (and accept it if there is), we'd never know how we're navigating through this world.

People also teach us about ourselves indirectly. Author and philosopher, Jim Rohn once said, "We are the average of the five people we spend the most time with." Who are your five people? What are their traits? What, in them, do you also see in yourself? What, in them, would you like to see in yourself? While we attract who we are, we also attract what we need.

Meditation: Close your eyes and try to tap in your seven-year-old self. What's precious about her? What do you love about her? Talk to her and listen to her.

LESSON 7

Women Need Each Other

"Always remember that your lips are stronger than his glue. And when you cannot budge, there are mouths that will vouch for you." - Spirit speaking through **Kennedy Engasser** (age 15 :: city 813)

Prompt: Think of someone who hurt you deeply—so deeply you don't even talk about it with just anyone (if anyone at all). Let's name this person "zero." Write a letter to "zero" and start it with, "I'm stronger." Now keep going.

Story: Tarana Burke's #MeToo movement was hella powerful. I wonder if she even knew it'd go that far. Celebrities and non-celebrities alike were being called out on their shit. Women who never spoke on the trauma against their bodies gained courage to speak. And the women who chose not to speak were still, in many ways, spoken for.

We choose not to speak about what happens to us for so many reasons. Sometimes it's embarrassing, or maybe we're not really clear on what exactly happened, or we feel that we share some of the blame. Then there's the fear of retaliation or isolation. And sometimes we just prefer to leave the past in the past. Whatever you choose, it's your right.

But if the experience is still bothering you—if it's still lingering in the back of your mind or your womb, whispering when you want it to shut up—consider that it might be time to talk about it. It might be sexual assault. It might be domestic violence. It might be verbal abuse. It might be neglect or abandonment. Whatever "it" is, if it still hurts, it wants to be addressed so that it can be released.

When we stuff it down and try to cover it up, it manifests in other ways, like addictions, illnesses, disorders, and self-sabotaging habits. You locked it in. To free it, you have to get it out. If it's hard to say, write it down first. Write it down then throw it in water or burn it or bury it. Then decide who you'll share it with. Never forget that a licensed therapist is always an option. But you're not alone. If #MeToo taught us nothing else, it's that we're not alone.

Meditation: Your best self lives without a lick of shame or guilt. Don't imagine her years from now; picture that glow on you right now. Now bring it from the mental to the physical. You can sing about it, write about it, draw it, paint it, dance while visualizing, and act it out— whatever you want! Just bring it to the physical, to the present.

LESSON 8

When the Future Seems Scary

"I've never heard anyone say they were scared of how big a tree would grow once they planted the seed. Being scared of opportunities that lie ahead are only preventing you from reaching success." - Spirit speaking through **McKenzie Harpe** (age 20 :: city 912)

> **Prompt:** Think of an opportunity that you had that scared you in the decision-making process. How did you respond? If you went for it anyway, despite your fear, write a letter to yourself for that brief moment when you were afraid. If you didn't do it, write a letter to yourself in which you forgive yourself (if necessary) and make a game plan for the next time a scary but exciting opportunity swings by.

Story: In a way, I feel like I grew up with a rich dad and a poor dad (if you're familiar with that book title). My biological dad wasn't rich, but he was and still is so ambitious. He'd mention an idea he had and then go for it. Sometimes he wouldn't even mention it; he'd just do it. From owning a restaurant to his own welding business to buying over twenty acres of land to eventually rent out, if an opportunity lights him up inside, he's going for it.

My stepdad, on the other, had so many great ideas that he never went for. There was the vending machine idea, the wine shop, the house flipping, etc. He'd collect all of these books on starting businesses and on saving and investing (hence how I learned about and read the book *Rich Dad, Poor Dad*), but he just never stuck his neck out there.

Thankfully, I took after my biological dad in this instance. Particularly after my stepdad passed away at 43 years old, I was hella motivated not to leave this earth full of wishes and wonders. In all of my experience going for it, the scariest part has always been right before I do it. Once I do it, I'm good. Leading up to it, though, I'm a nervous wreck.

Don't let that fear paralyze you. Don't dismiss your fear either, because it definitely serves a purpose. Acknowledge it and what it's trying to tell you, and then respond. My fear of quitting my job and working for myself was that I might fail (and I have bills). So I responded to my fear: if I fail, I'll get another job and try again later.

Meditation: Go for a walk outdoors. While out, say, "I owe it to myself to _____, despite _____," filling the blanks with what you feel appropriate. Keep going until you're either out of things to say or you've completed your walk. Close it with a prayer.

LESSON 9

Acceptance and Evolution

"Self-reflection brings so much into light that you've allowed to be left in the dark." - Spirit speaking through **Vanessa "Moral" Maldonado** (age 20 :: city 469)

Prompt: Write down twenty-one things you love about your *self* (the inner you). Then write down another twenty-one things you love about yourself (the outer you). If you ain't yet arrived at loving yet, just write down what you accept about yourself.

Story: To get through shit, we sometimes have to pack it away. We don't have the time or the ability to deal with it right then and there. We pack away joy, too. We get caught up in life's matrix, in the rat race, and we leave behind what makes us happy. We're so driven to accomplish, to make others happy, and to get from this point to that one. In doing so, we miss out on so much peace of mind and potential for growth.

Vanessa said, "You are not the person you were one year ago, three years ago, or five years ago. Your life is not what you thought it would be. But you are still here. Remind yourself that, even if you have lived a lifetime's worth of trauma at a young age, you cannot abandon the rest of your life. You have to remain curious.

"Stagnancy is like quicksand. After everything that's happened, what's next? Fucking bring it. You've never had a say, so take it back. Make it yours. Make it something you don't have to survive. Make it something you wish you could stop time for. One truth I've come to trust is that life is about experience. Watch for those moments you can stop, and realize this is one of them. You won't realize how special it is until it's a memory."

Meditation: Take a moment to bask in your glory. From your toes up to your calves, knees, hips, torso, chest, arms, hands, collarbones, nose, eyes, and scalp. The energy you radiate and the love you vibrate—swim in that light. Settle into your magnificence.

LESSON 10

Stop Sleeping on Yourself

"Being authentic means being true to yourself, meaning you don't cap your potential to protect anyone's feelings. You're raw as fuck." - Spirit speaking through **Breyauna Nelson** (age 20 :: 410)

> **Prompt**: When are you most yourself? When do you feel you're not being yourself? What do you wish you did more often? Write about it.

Story: As we all are, I was a completely different person between the ages of seventeen and twenty-one than I am now. I was rough around the edges; didn't trust many people; juggled about three different dudes at once; and I spent most of my money on clothes, weed, food, nails, and my hair. The problem was I was also late on bills every single month. My friends matched that energy.

Then I started going to the gym to get a big butt and a flat stomach. Later, I saw an ad about a yoga class. I went and loved it. Then I started meditating. Then I started reading my Bible again. I wasn't interested in clubbing as often. I got tired of being broke all the time, so I started spending my money differently. I wouldn't tell a lot of people about these changes though, because I didn't want them looking at me differently or laughing it off.

I didn't even realize I was capping my potential around certain people until I stopped spending as much time with them. In retrospect, there were two red flags: 1) I didn't share what I was creatively or spiritually working on with them, and 2) I downplayed my successes around them. Your good news ain't bragging; it's just your truth. Mike Tyson once said in an interview, and I'm paraphrasing, that confidence comes off as arrogance to an insecure person.

Big up yourself! Breyauna said, "Be raw, real and relatable. Not seeking approval from anyone. Empowering others while being content with your being. Growing with every experience. Being able to be courageous. Not being perfect, but being okay with your mistakes. Accepting the curves life throws at you. Being okay with yourself despite others' opinions. Accepting flaws. Being authentic, because the last thing this planet needs is more fake people."

Meditation: The chakra system was created in India before the Common Era. Energy leaves and enters your body through chakras. We have seven main ones. They're counted from the bottom up. The root chakra, the first one, pertains to your sense of security and confidence, and it's located just below your tailbone. For one minute, bring your attention there. Sit on your hands if it helps. Now verbally declare everything that you are, starting with "I am."

LESSON 11

Having Faith While Changing the Game

"Say a prayer, then say, 'Fuck it.'" - Spirit speaking through **Raya Tuffaha** (age 20 :: city 206)

Prompt: The first few lines of the Bible's serenity prayer reads, "God, grant me the serenity to accept the things I cannot change, the courage to change the things I can, and the wisdom to know the difference." Activist and writer Angela Davis tweaked that prayer and wrote, "I am no longer accepting the things I cannot change. I am changing the things I cannot accept." In this moment, which one resonates with you most? Set a timer for seven minutes; choose one of the quotes, read it three times, then write whatever comes up for you.

Story: I first learned about the serenity prayer in middle school. I was in the assistant principal's office being sent home for something I'd gotten in trouble for. (I don't remember what, and I don't know why a prayer was posted in a public school.) I just knew my ass was grass when I got home, because it was the second time that month that my parents had been called. Yet the deed was done. I couldn't do anything about it at that point. As the prayer suggested, since I couldn't change it, I'd *mize well* accept it. I shrugged it off and took whatever was coming to me.

I carried that mindset on through my teenage years and into my adulthood too. That ain't to say that I ain't never been phased by nothing.

That's far from the truth. But when I find myself overwhelmed with anxiety and worry, it usually somehow comes to mind all on its own. Control what you can; never mind what you can't.

Raya's quote works for both the Bible's version of the serenity prayer and Angela's. Sometimes the battle ain't worth fighting or worrying about. Say a prayer and then say *fuck it*. Other times, you gotta pull your sleeves up and demand a better experience for yourself and/or your people. Pray. Fuck whatever fears come up for you, and do what you gotta do.

Meditation: Every day, usually before bed, but sometimes earlier if I'm stressed, I do three things: 1) Unplug. I turn off my phone to get away from the emails, texts, and social media notifications. I keep it off either for the rest of the night or for a few hours. 2) Give myself permission to stop thinking about one thing. It's hard to say stop worrying or thinking about *everything*. One thing is much easier. And it's like instant relief. 3) Find pleasure. Dance, read, watch TV, journal, take a nap, pleasure myself sexually, something. Try those three things for yourself for your meditation today.

LESSON 12

Affirmations when it's Hard to Hold On

"Stop. Breathe. You will be all right. Just hold on for now so we can smile later." - Spirit speaking through Jayla (age 18 :: city 912)

Prompt: We gotta pat ourselves on the back. We don't do that enough. Think of three things you accomplished already. It could be a big thing like graduating high school or a small thing like getting out of bed this morning. Five years ago or five minutes ago. Don't overthink it. Just write, "Good job for _____." Fill in the blank with three things. Then write, "Good job for working on _____." Fill in the blank with three things you're working toward.

Story: When I was fourteen I wanted to kill myself. Plain and simple. But the turmoil I held inside made days of sadness seem like weeks on end. Until they turned into months. Then years. Then everything became numb. Became hot. Angry. Depressed. Disheartened.

The world stopped moving. I was choosing my next landmark. A period or semicolon. To end it all or take a pause. To be here or there. To take my last breath unfulfilled or carry out my will to be here writing for the next girl struggling to hang on.

To reach out. I know it's awkward, even uncomfortable, but damn it's gon' feel 'bout good as hell. So please cry, snot-nosed and all. Please yell with all the voice cracks, stutters, and emphases you can imagine. The beauty comes in your own healing. So do whatever you need to get back to yourself.

Meditation: If you're feeling numb or depressed or hopeless, here's some free confidential counseling: Call the NAMI Helpline at 800-950-6264 M-F, 10:00 a.m. – 6:00 p.m., ET. If you're in a crisis, text "NAMI" to 741741 for 24/7, confidential, free crisis counseling.

If that's not your current mental and emotional state, then let's make a plan. Emotions can be so unpredictable. It's best to be prepared. Let's get your toolbox ready now. What's your first line of defense? Is there a song that lifts you up? An activity that brightens your day? What can you do to recharge your spirit with hope? Now let's consider the second line of defense, in case the first ain't enough. Do you have a friend you trust to listen to you, and also be compassionate and honest? This person should feel comfortable and be able to tell you to get professional help, if necessary. The third line should always be professional help. Hotlines like NAMI and 211 are great options. Having a therapist already researched and lined up is a great idea too. Many offer sliding scale payment options, taking whatever you can afford.

LESSON 13

I Am My Own Standard of Beauty

"What helped me be at peace with my body was understanding the system that I was comparing it to is marginalized, un-inclusive, and controlled by patriarchal and capitalist, colorist values." - Spirit speaking through **Alexis Taylor** (age 20 :: city 313)

Prompt: We tend to think of imagination as something for children. It's for everybody though. It's especially for those who are oppressed (at some kind of disadvantage as a result of who they are and how they show up in the world). Before change can happen, it has to be imagined first. So set an alarm for eleven minutes and imagine the world you'd like to live in. How would this one need to be changed? Get radical with it. Be bold.

Story: Have you ever taken time to stand in your mirror naked? Purposefully and not just during the quick moments between hitting the shower? Bare and vulnerable. Not from any flattering angles, no sucking in nothing. What do you see?

When I first tried this, I imagined what Eve must have felt like. Self-aware and accepting of her physical being. I wondered if she took the moment to examine herself in some body of water. But what would be the reason?

I stared at that girl standing across from me apathetically, and she stared back at me. Her arms rose to disproportionate cleavage, traced the blemishes about our stomach, and then greeted our dimpled hips, which complemented our backside. I looked down to darkened knees and ankles, and acknowledged the scars of every color on our legs. (We had a fun childhood.) Her fingernails left tire marks from old bug bites and eczema flare ups, and her back flaunted its pair of twin rolls.

There we stood. Pigeon-toed, flabby-armed, and content. I am my own standard of beauty.

Meditation: Stand in front of a mirror as naked as you can safely challenge yourself to. If total nudity is too uncomfortable, wear underwear. If that's too uncomfortable, keep your clothes on. Challenge yourself though. Study your body. Look in your eyes. Point out areas that stand out to you, especially the parts you don't care for. This ain't to get you to love every part of your body or even to accept it. In this meditation, we're going to tell every part of your body that it deserves to be loved. That's all. (Stomach, you deserve to be loved. Stretch marks, you deserve to be loved. Flabby arms, you deserve to be loved. Half-painted toes, you deserve to be loved. Wide nose, you deserve to be loved.) Go for it.

LESSON 14

The Beauty in the Bad

"Yes, my home life isn't the best, my mental health is not always in good shape, and I struggle with body weight issues. But I used those moments to FUEL ME and help me grow." - Spirit speaking through Na'Erykah (age 18 :: city 912)

> **Prompt**: Make a list of ten things you've overcome/survived in your life. Being bullied in third grade counts just as much as life-threatening illnesses or incidents.

Story: Testimonies were one of my favorite parts of church growing up. I used to boo-hoo cry hearing about women, in particular, talk about everything they been through and how they didn't think they'd make it, and yet they're here to tell their stories. That never gets old. It's amazing what we're capable of surviving. The things meant to destroy us, and that have taken other people out, we overcame.

No one really knows what you go through like you do. Despite your insecurities and mental/physical challenges, you keep showing up. We all have our shit. When rich people say money can't buy happiness, that's what they're saying: we all have our shit. We all have difficult memories, regrets, insecurities, struggles, and battles. None outweighs the other. All of it is difficult, and it's impossible to dodge everything. Something will latch on and get to you. You may as well let it fuel you. Cry when you need to cry. Scream when you need to scream. Roll your eyes at it. Cuss it. But keep going. Use it to manifest a life beyond your wildest dreams.

Meditation: Intentionally finding beauty in things helps you see the beauty in (almost) everything. If you can, take a walk outside for however long you're in the mood for. If you can only muster the energy to stand in one place outdoors, that's fine too. If going to the window is all you got in you, that's cool too. Once you're in place, pay attention to things you'd ordinarily overlook and find something beautiful about them. Challenge yourself. Get creative.

LESSON 15

Uncovering Self-Validation among Naysayers

"Refuse to confuse desire with necessity, especially when it comes to being understood." - Spirit speaking through Trelani Michelle (age 32 :: city 504)

> **Prompt**: At the top of your page, write the following: "I desire to be understood, however ..." Complete your thought.

Story: Writer and feminist Gloria Steinem read the words off my heart when she said that being misunderstood by people whose opinions you value is absolutely the most painful experience. When I sent my debut novel, *What the Devil Meant for Bad*, to authors whose opinions I very much valued, at least half of them told me it wasn't a good idea. They weren't saying there were holes in my plot or that my characters weren't fully developed; they were telling me to soften the edges.

Because it was Christian-based, they felt that I needed to remove the profanity and sex scenes. However, to do that would have meant altering the way that Spirit gave the story to me. The mere thought of doing so made me feel like I was being unfaithful to myself. I couldn't allow their well-meaning opinions to redirect my purpose.

Maybe you were outright rejected, ignored, or discouraged. Self-validation is key in the path of enlightenment. If you aren't careful, naysayers will have you thinking your truth is insufficient and your perspective is off. The last word is always yours. When you find yourself in that space again, repeat the prompt.

Meditation: Briskly rub your hands together to heat 'em up. Begin massaging your abdomen, above your belly button (solar plexus) and below it (sacral chakra) to activate and enhance your personal power, self-esteem, and confidence.

LESSON 16

Bouncing Back After A Heartbreak

"Get better, baby. Don't get bitter and damn sho don't beg." - Spirit speaking through Trelani Michelle (age 32 :: city 504)

> **Prompt**: Have you ever had your heart broken? By a family member, friend, or lover? Did you talk down on yourself afterwards (or compare yourself or wish you were somehow better)? Write down the negative things you thought/wondered about yourself. Then scratch each one out and replace it with compliments fit for a god.

Story: My first heartbreak was around fourteen. My "best friend" called and made me promise not to get mad for what she was about to tell me. She had not only had sex with the guy whose babies I wanted to have, but she had lost her virginity with him. I pretended not to be mad, but I think that made it worse.

My second heartbreak was at eighteen by my son's father, and the next was at twenty-one by my daughter's father. I think somewhere along the line, I started expecting it. I'd get mad but never surprised. That's when I realized that beneath the forgiveness (and retaliation), I was bitter as hell. I had to let that go, but before I could, I had to figure out why I had hoarded all of these heartbreaks. Why was I still carrying the hurt from ages fourteen and eighteen, into my twenties and thirties?

The "aha" moment was that each time it happened, I questioned myself. I stood in the mirror and picked myself to pieces. Maybe if my hair was softer, my teeth straighter, my shoulders slimmer, my butt bigger. Maybe if I wasn't so serious all the time. Then I realized that their cheating really wasn't about me. As much as my ego wanted me to believe it was, it wasn't. They didn't do it to make me sad or mad. They were just doing them. That didn't align with what I wanted in a relationship, though. So it didn't make sense to keep tearing myself down every time I didn't feel chosen. I started noticing how I changed many of my ways to be super compatible. Instead, I started reclaiming what I actually liked and was curious about. I started dating, dressing up, going out, prioritizing my personal goals—and feeling good again. It took time, but I got better.

Like Nala from DC said best, "You will start to be better. You will start to feel better and receive an 'I miss you' that will be translated to 'I tried to find someone better, and I couldn't.' It's like an elevator. You can either stop to let them back in or keep moving up."

Meditation: The compliments you wrote during the writing prompt, take 'em out. Stand in front of the mirror and repeat each one to yourself until you damn near (or do) memorize 'em.

LESSON 17

The Value of Experience

"Stop wishing for money and start praying for the things you want to do with the money." - Spirit speaking through Trelani (age 32 :: city 504)

Prompt: How much money would be a super duper blessing to you right now? Write that number at the top of the page. Now make a list of everything you want to do with that money. No shame in it either—even if it's $50,000 worth of shoes. It's your money and your list.

Story: Whenever the clocks changes to 11:11, my daughter and I make a wish. For the longest time, my wish was always to have more money. I'd want $10,000 before the month ended, a million by my next birthday, or even just the funds to be able to pay my car note on time that month.

One day, while meditating, I realized that I *was* making more money. In a span of seven years, I went from making $7 an hour to $15 an hour to $40,000 a year to $60,000 a year. I still wanted more money though, and I didn't want that to continue being my pattern. I didn't want to start making $100,000 and then wish for more. Making a million and then wish for more. I ain't wanna be one of those rich people who preached that money couldn't buy happiness.

God asked what I wanted to do with the money, and I rambled off a list: I wanna travel more (and with my children too), to not have to worry about if I'll be able to pay the bills on time, to be able to treat myself to new clothes and shoes whenever I want, a bunch of plants and homemade beauty products, a chef and a maid, and I want to buy houses all over the world for women to be able to go to, be safe at, and create or just rest.

Then those things started showing up. No lie. That same summer, I visited over fifteen cities in Georgia, Tennessee, Texas, Louisiana, Alabama, and Michigan. Baby, I was exhausted from those two road trips, and instead of having to spend money to go, I was paid to go. I started getting more t-shirts by black-owned creators and the plants and the homemade beauty products. I told a chef I followed on Instagram how much I wanted him to cook for me one day. He said, "Next time you're in New Orleans, let me know. I love your work and would love to cook for you."

Mind blown.

So yeah, I don't pray for money no mo. I ask for what I want instead. Sounds crazy, I know, but money can get in the way sometimes. With the houses all over the world, for instance, if I waited until I had the money to make that happen, who knows when it would? When I started to focus on the desire, however, it was simple math. I rented a big-ass house on Hilton Head beach for me and six other women to go and create and rest for a whole weekend.

Meditation: When you think of having a lot of money, however much that is to you, what do you look forward to the most? Set a timer for three minutes, place one hand over your heart and the other just below your belly button, close your eyes, and visualize yourself experiencing whatever it is you most look forward to.

LESSON 18

Interest vs. Intention

"I promised my soul I'd stop making myself an extracurricular activity. Neglecting to turn on the light doesn't mean it's not there. The motion to do so just hasn't been initiated." - Spirit speaking through Sierra Vincent (age 20 :: city 912)

> **Prompt:** In what area of your life do you make the most excuses? What's the truth of the matter? How can you either step into your truth or remove yourself from the situation?
>
> Write about it.

Story: One of the best things I could have possibly done for my clients (and myself) was help them figure out if finishing their book was an interest or an intention. This goes for you and your ambitions, too. If you're interested, you may very well still do it—if it's convenient. If it's your intention, then you're committed and will make room for it. You'll do what it takes to make it happen.

I first put off writing my book because I'd just had a baby and decided to wait until he got a little older. By the time he got a little older, I was in college and working full-time. I realized then that there would always be a reason not to write my book. My excuses were valid, but if I didn't find a way to work around my excuses, then I'd never accomplish my goal.

One thing about an excuse is that we usually test it out on ourselves before we try to sell it to others. We mention the excuse in passing to see if we receive validation, pity, sympathy, or empathy.

Instead of making an excuse, make a choice. This means the reason you didn't get something done was because you chose not to do it. It's saying that, in spite of a long-ass to-do list and everything going on around you (and maybe even inside of you), you're holding yourself accountable. Distinguish between the interests and the intentions. If it was and still is an intention, recommit to it. That's a big-girl-panty-wearing move right there.

You made a commitment, and then something came up. Life happened. What you gon' do?

Meditation: Take a few minutes to stretch. While doing so, say, "I owe it to myself to _____, in spite of _____," filling the blanks with what you feel appropriate. Keep going until you're either out of things to say or you've completed your stretch. Close it with a prayer.

LESSON 19

Making Peace When It's Time to Go

"I'm starting to love the sound of my feet when I am walking away from things that are no longer meant for me." - Spirit speaking through **Nala** (age 18 :: city 202)

> **Prompt:** There's a quote that floats around social media that says, "Let go or be dragged." The letting go might be temporary or permanent. Might be releasing a person, a thought, a habit, etc. Think back to a time when you pursued something or someone for too long. On paper, rewrite the story where you leave or stop before it becomes a real problem.

Story: When I first started high school, I couldn't wait for all the basketball games, pool parties, and sleepovers with a girl group I'd be together with all four years. My middle school years can kiss my ass 'cause I still cringe thinking about all the lil "phases" I went through. So now that I'd changed my personality for the umpteenth time, my first couple of weeks were dedicated to scouting for my perfectly imperfect people, starting with a girl I'd met in the eighth grade.

A friendship I'd had since elementary school ended in middle school. It wasn't too surprising, considering we'd been off and on in seventh grade. But it still hurt, because I considered her my best friend, and she'd started acting real mean. And I wasn't with that. We had different opinions on things, and I felt she was too negative too often. In eighth grade, I cut it off altogether. I was going through a lot in my personal life and didn't have any room for extra confusion or chaos. We had several mutual friends, and she basically outed me from the group. They took sides, and they all chose her. On top of battling depression, I also had to deal with gossip about me from people I once considered friends.

Quasia, who also contributed her thoughts to this book, said it best: "It's important to get clarity on where you stand with a person. 'Friend' to you can mean 'associate' to them." And something I am still learning to accept about myself is that I was not made to fit in, and where I am right now is where I am supposed to be. Though hurtful, that situation was necessary. It taught me a lot—about friendship, about myself, and the importance of walking away from things that are no longer meant for me.

Meditation: Every autumn, the earth sheds what it no longer needs. Fallen leaves, for instance, decompose and nourish the soil. That isn't meaningless; it serves its purpose. What is it time for you to release? Place your hands over your heart, close your eyes, and picture what you need to let go of. Thank it for however it's served you up to this point, and then verbally tell it that its time is done.

LESSON 20

Forgiving Yourself

"It took a long time to learn, but I know how to forgive myself. Every time I have to, I remind myself that without forgiving me, I can't move on. And if I can't move on from my past, I'm robbing the world of any light I can bring in my future." - Spirit speaking through Leilani (age 19 :: city 240)

Prompt: Maya Angelou once said, "You can't forgive without loving. And I don't mean sentimentality. I don't mean mush. I mean having enough courage to stand up and say, 'I forgive. I'm finished with it.'" At the top of your paper, write "I'm finished with it." Now list everything you're ready to be done with. Consider thoughts that run through your mind, memories that replay at night, experiences that disrupt your ability to trust others, etc.

Story: When my parents split up, I felt their quarrel was bound to find its way into the lives of my siblings and me. They were living in separate houses for one, and conversations mentioning "divorce" and "adult" were always within ears reach (and I was nosy). Since they were divorced most of my life, I tried to keep both halves of my heart happy. I just didn't expect to have to be pressured to *love* one parent over the other.

Meditation: Most breathing techniques ask you to breathe in and out through your nose, but for this one, breathe in through your nose and out through your mouth. When you inhale—and take your time with it—consider what you need to forgive yourself for. When you exhale, visualize your breath carrying that forgiveness out of your lungs and into your heart. If there's someone else you'd like to forgive, repeat the exercise with their offense in mind.

LESSON 21

The Pleasure & Power in Saying No

"Forgetting how to say no after being labeled 'bossy' or a 'b*tch' becomes one of the easiest or the hardest things to do. Say no. If they don't like it, they'll get to stepping. Saying no protects you." - Spirit speaking through **Jordan (age 18 :: city 912)**

> **Prompt:** At the top of your paper, write the following: "I'm not
> _____, but I _____." What have you been called that you
> don't agree with? Write that in the first line. In place of what you've
> been called, write what you actually claim for yourself in the
> second line. For example, "I'm not stuck up, but I do have
> standards." Repeat until you're out of names you've been called.

Story: Sexual energy is creative energy, since both are housed in the sacral chakra. When this channel is imbalanced, you might find yourself:

- people pleasing without minding your own feelings;

- feeling emotionally detached from yourself and those around you;

- feeling under-stimulated;

- suffering from a creative block; or

- letting yourself go (whatever that means for you).

Oh, but when it's popping?! You are:

- genuinely happy;

- confident regardless of others' opinions;

- aware of how you want to feel and what you want to experience;

- okay with telling others no;

- tuned in to your creativity; and

- feeling overall balanced.

Engaging in sensual activities is the best way to keep your sacral chakra open and happy. Sensual activities include getting sunlight and fresh air, dressing without panties, mindfully eating raw fruits and veggies, listening to live music, drinking hot tea, getting massages, involving yourself in stimulating conversations, and engaging in shameless, unrushed solo sex sessions. Fall in love with your precious parts— again. They ain't just for making babies and pleasing others. They're for you. For your pleasure and power. Go ahead, love. Tune in.

Meditation: Yoni breathing brings awareness to the pelvic area, deepens your personal relationship, and enhances your creative energy. *Really* step into your power by adding an affirmation. Slowly inhale while contracting your pelvic floor muscles (the same muscles you use to hold your pee). Hold for three to five seconds (longer if you can) while visualizing your affirmation, and then slowly release. Note: Make sure your throat, jaw and mouth are relaxed, since they are directly connected to the hips and precious parts.

LESSON 22

A Love Unchanging

"Questioning your sexuality is hard, especially when you live in the South. I had friends and adults tell me loving the same sex is a sin and I would end up in hell. What I've learned is that love is the most powerful thing in this world. God will love you no matter what." - Spirit speaking through **Anonymous**

Prompt: What were you taught about sex? What attitudes and beliefs were conveyed to you by the adults in your life, school, and church? Which of these attitudes and beliefs did you internalize? Write about it.

Story: Niobe Anyanwu, aka Ashley Bernadette, repping the 313, is holding down this entire story: "One of the places I still despise attending is the church (the Kingdom Hall too). Ironically, I lament the idea of crossing man-engineered holy gates. I've felt this way prior to being supposedly 'woke.'

Having to put on this self-righteous marquee is just not authentic for me, and I didn't stop wearing weaves just to lace some high-riding holy rollers with a front regarding who I AM.

I'm not gonna act like I'm always choosing the teachings of Christ over a Jhené Aiko track to get me through. I'm not gonna act like sex is taboo, although I'm not married. And I for damn sure will not act as though *shit, fuck*, and *this bitch* don't exit my lips when communicating to God what angsts me. Surely, I'm no saint—and don't wanna be.

All I wish to be is free. Free to express without fishing for words that comfort them and they. A total suppression of what would potentially set me free.

I'm not trying to be perfect; I'm trying to be free."

Meditation: Place your hands over your throat. Don't choke yourself though. Just lay your hands there. Repeat this powerful affirmation by Auset "Settie" Lee, "I told lies of who I was and who I be, just so I could make people proud of who they wanted to really see. But over time I realized that God was the only one who could judge me. And for that, I relearned how to love me." Repeat this, if you want, but customize it. Make it more personal and exact for you.

LESSON 23

Know-it-Alls and Feeling Small

"Everybody's struggle and story is different. So where you are right now is exactly where you need to be." - Spirit speaking through Aakiryah (age 19 :: city 202)

Prompt: Make a list of fifty things you're grateful for about yourself (e.g., how strong you are) and your life (e.g., you have a friend who really gives a damn about you).

Story: I met a guy on a poetry tour. I was attracted to his confidence but quickly learned that it was really arrogance. He told me one day that he doesn't touch people he looks up to because he can grow from them. "For people like you," he said to me, "I don't really feel threatened. I'm not calling you dumb though." I had to make sure I heard that right. Like, *boy ... what?*

There will always be people who think they know it all, and it's important not to let their big words or their life experiences make you feel small. Everybody's struggle and story are different. They may know more about a particular subject than you do, but you also know more than them on some other subject.

I remember visiting the civil rights museum in Savannah with members of my class. One of the guys from Atlanta said that Savannah's museum was "unnecessary"; he didn't learn anything because he didn't feel that the information pertained to him. While it's true that Atlanta's museum is most likely bigger than Savannah's, that doesn't make it better—just different. They're two different experiences.

Someone who's already visited ten different countries ain't better than the person who's never left their state. The girl who's been in the same relationship for the past five years ain't better than the girl whose longest relationship was a month. Curly hair ain't better than coily, and thick ain't better than slim. It's just different. Anyone who thinks otherwise is close-minded and missing out on some really valuable lessons, experiences, and connections.

Where you are right now, what you know right now, and what you've done so far are all good. You're right where you're supposed to be. And if someone sees a problem with that—especially if they try to make you see a problem with that—then you should reconsider how much you engage with that person.

Meditation: Practice a moving meditation this time. Dance, draw, go for a walk, clean your room, take a shower, etc. While you're doing it, repeat to yourself, "I'm right where I'm supposed to be. Despite feeling like I should be _____ by now, I'm right where I'm supposed to be."

LESSON 24

Dreams + Expectations = WTF Do I Do?

"You said I can be anything, but I heard 'You have to be everything.' So I always feel stuck trying to change myself for you." - Spirit speaking through **Kennedi Jordan** (age 17 :: city 912)

Prompt: At the top of your paper, write the following: "The thought of it scares and excites me at the same time." What is "it" for you? Why does it scare and excite you? Write about it.

Story: The whole gifted program in elementary school? I was a part of that. In kindergarten, my dad would send me a first grade math book to do in class on top of the kindergarten work. Then he called my teacher to check my work for me. There was this expectation on me to be the best. To be better than everyone else around me. To work two times as hard. The pressure was always on, so I figured out how to survive whatever environments and challenges I was faced with. I did so well that I never had to study in elementary or middle school. Then when it came time to critically think through problems, I found myself stuck. I can solve this three-foot long math problem, but I struggle to think through real-life situations.

"You can be anything you want to be when you grow up." That's what they say out of one side of their mouth. Out of the other side, they're rushing you to choose and pointing out jobs that pay a lot of money. It's hard to remember what I ate for breakfast or what I want to eat for lunch, let alone choosing what I want to do with the rest of my life at sixteen, seventeen, or eighteen years old. And in all those subtle ways, we're reminded of the sacrifices made for us. We're reminded of what's on the line. We don't want to disappoint. We're so accustomed to being the star student, and it can be overwhelming sometimes.

For once, I don't wanna concern myself with what makes everyone else happy. I don't want to spend the rest of my life trying to make and keep other people proud of me. I'm tired of competing. I want the space to make mistakes and try again. I want space to be average sometimes. Find what excites me and go after with my whole heart until I change my mind and want to try something else.

Meditation: The prompt called for you to write out one of your scary-exciting desires. Now meditate on it. Close your eyes and see it. Feel it. Bring it from the space of *maybe* to the place of *yes*.

LESSON 25

When There's No Room at the Table ...

"You got me fucked up if you think I'ma shrink myself to be more palatable for someone else. Any space I take up belongs to me, and that's how I gotta live." - Spirit speaking through Avery Owens (age 18 :: city 443)

> **Prompt:** Consider the people in your life, your environments, and the habits you own that don't align with your values. How do you plan to distance yourself from these bad vibes?

Write about it.

Story: No one had ever taught me how to express my emotions, particularly anger. As a result, I became very passive-aggressive, especially in my romantic relationships. Because I also had low self-esteem, my inability to express myself made me depressed, possessive, jealous, and dishonest. To cover up, I used sex as a tactic, along with inauthentic "friendly" gestures and favors. In return, I had high expectations, and whenever life didn't go right, I had something or someone to blame. I was miserable.

Being passive-aggressive is likely a result of having experienced oppression. Ironically, passive-aggression is a form of oppression. It consists of feeling restrained, limited, silenced, exploited, abused, and marginalized. Recognizing this helps us better identify it. Recognizing your own personality type can help you determine how you end up in toxic environments and ultimately how to avoid or solve them.

The opposite of passive-aggression is assertion. This is also the best way to deal with oppressive people, environments, and habits. Assertion doesn't mean you aren't afraid. It means that, despite the chin trembles, tears, and deep breaths, you stand up for yourself, speak your mind and your truth, respectfully and straightforwardly ask for what you want, and make yourself willing to let someone go for the sake of your inner peace. It doesn't matter if it's a customer, family member, friend, spouse, supervisor, or mirror reflection. It's standing up to whoever and saying, as Avery said best, "I belong wherever I decide, and no one is ever going to convince me otherwise."

Meditation: Your throat chakra has everything to do with taking responsibility for your needs, being willing to express yourself in all circumstances. Your hips are directly connected to your throat. Moving your hips can clear your throat chakra and give you assertive power. Research hip-opening yoga poses and try a few, or turn on some music and move those hips!

LESSON 26

Solitude within Self-care

"It's okay to be by yourself." - Spirit speaking through **Raven (age 17 ::
city 386)**

> **Prompt:** Set a date with yourself—within your means, of course. If
> you have access to transportation, cool. If not, cool. Do something
> that you used to love but haven't done in a while. Or try something
> that you've been wanting to do with someone else or that you
> usually do with someone else, by yourself.

Story: From the time we enter daycare or school, we're shown that it's
not okay to be by yourself. If you were caught standing alone in a corner
or playing by yourself with the blocks, the teacher would either come
over and join you or push another loner off on you. They meant well,
but what happened is that they taught you that we need the company of
others.

Connection is a critical part of the human experience. We need each
other, no doubt. But we also need alone time. Some of us need solitude
more than others. Sometimes, it's because of our personalities and what
we need to recharge. Other times, it's because of what we're going
through emotionally.

The best distinction I've ever read regarding introverts and extroverts
went something like this: introverts don't necessarily prefer to be alone

or not know how to engage with others without being awkward. It's just that when they're mentally exhausted or overwhelmed, they need solitude to recharge. Extroverts, on the other hand, need to be around other people to recharge. That description worked so much better than what I'd been taught beforehand.

I learned that solitude was one of the best remedies for confusion back when I was eighteen years old. My roommate and I had just split, so I was working two jobs to be able to afford rent and my car note alone. My three-year relationship had not too long ago ended, and my heart was still in shambles. My friends at the time wanted to go out every single weekend, and, to be honest, I was exhausted. But I didn't want to seem like a loser who couldn't get over her ex-boyfriend. I didn't feel attractive. My finances were shot. My wardrobe sucked. I no longer knew what I wanted to do with my future. And though I was surrounded by plenty of people, I still felt lonely. I'd say I was misunderstood, but I don't even think I understood my damn self.

I was severely depressed. In some form or fashion, I ended up pushing everyone away. I didn't have cable, and social media wasn't popping like it is today (in fact, Facebook was only for college students at that time), so I had few distractions. I started journaling and praying. I realized that it was sink or swim. I started setting goals and doing shit that I used to love (like scrapbooking). I started writing down what I wanted and needed out of romantic relationships and friendships. I started thinking back on past situations that hurt like hell, not to depress myself even more but to figure out what I could've done differently to leave me with less regret.

I also realized that I needed to go back home. It sucked to have to move back in with my mom, but it was in my best interest. Without rent and utilities to stress about every month, I had even more space to think clearly and design a life for myself that felt satisfying. And I did just that.

Without that alone time, though, I don't think I would've gotten to that point.

These days, I still prioritize alone time. But I'm more proactive about it. I grab it before I'm starving for it. And it shows in the health of my relationships, the glow in my skin, and the progress of my creativity.

Meditation: Our third eye is located between our brows. It is our ability to recognize kindred (and non-kindred) spirits, show compassion, and act in our truth. When our third eye is blocked, we have trouble sleeping, feel anxious and irritable, feel creatively blocked, and have a worse-than-normal memory. When it's open, though, we're connected to our intuition and creativity. One way to open and balance this chakra is through a Third-eye Meditation.

Consciously release all tension in your body through slow, deep breaths. Once relaxed, imagine an indigo ball of light radiating between your brows. Inhale balance, clarity, and knowing. Exhale confusion, disconnect, and indecisiveness. Repeat this for three minutes.

LESSON 27

Hopelessness, Help, and Healing

"Being okay with getting help is like a weight lifted off your shoulders. Even though you may be dealing with it alone, you know somebody's there to help you through it." - Spirit speaking through **Imani** (age 13 :: city 912)

> **Prompt**: Write the words you need to hear.

Story: When I began my first year of college at Savannah State, I was ready for the busy class weeks; the Uno, danced-filled weekends; and the luxury of naps during the "school day" again. This was the freedom I had craved since living under my parents' roofs, so it was my responsibility to mother myself as best I could.

Since it's the end of 2020, my freshman year experience has been a lot more reserved compared to previous years. Most of my classes are online and my professors haven't been *too* unreasonable on the schoolwork (yet). Even though I knew that my college experience would be different, I wasn't looking over my shoulder for any more drastic life changes.

And that's when I got that phone call. My half-brother had overdosed in his trailer truck. It was my second week of classes. August 27th. I froze on the walk back to my dorm room. It was around 1:45 and I had a class at 2:00. I couldn't go. All I could do was cry for all of the "shouldas, wouldas, and couldas."

It took about a week for me to collect myself again. Dr. Carolyn Jordan, my freshman honors professor, allowed me the time, space, and support I needed. The members of my class even came together to gift their love and support as well. I was feeling better again.

And that's when I got that phone call. My best friend had passed away— on the *one* day I didn't check on his health. I completely fell apart. Deadlines from school and work brushed my shoulder without a glance. It even became hard to eat, drink, and just function in general.

Dr. Jordan came to my side once again. While on her way to a conference in New England, she stayed on the phone with me until she was sure I was okay. The next day, she referred me to the counseling department at SSU, where Ms. Jacqueline Awe serves as director on a board of willing ears.

Though friends and family offered support after each instance, I don't like bothering people with my own issues. But after talking through my feelings, my spirit felt lighter. I was no longer congested with suppressed sadness, anger, and every other emotion I can't put a name to. This was my first time grieving and my last time trying to face it alone.

Meditation: Here's a meditation that I do when my mind is super active and busy, and when I'm feeling really anxious. You'll literally watch your mind slow down. You need a timer, a notebook, and a pen. There are three rounds. For the first round, meditate for one minute. When the alarm goes off, make a list of every thought you had during that minute (or at least the thoughts you remember having). For the second round, meditate for three minutes. When the alarm goes off, make a list of every thought you had. For the last round, meditate for seven minutes. When the alarm goes off, make a list of every thought you had.

LESSON 28

Prove Yourself Wrong the Right Way

"I didn't think I could do it ... 'til I did it." - Spirit speaking through **Jayla**
(age 18 :: city 912)

> **Prompt**: Write about an experience that called for immediate action or insurgency that you followed through on, one that you're proud of. Include who, what, when, where, how, and why from the experience. Go so deep into the memory that you feel it in your body.

Story: I didn't think I could travel outside of the country by myself until I did it. They said it wasn't safe for a woman. I didn't think I could leave my marriage. They said I wouldn't find better. Didn't think I could tell my mom how she hurt me. They said I was being dramatic because it could've been worse. Didn't think I could move to the DC/Maryland/Virginia area (DMV). They said the cost of living was double. Didn't think I could become a runner or a plant mom or a public speaker. Thank God I was born with the spirit to do what the fuck I want to do, scared or not.

"We are told to act like adults, but we're treated like children. We voice our concerns, but no one will hear them. We are told that we are stupid, too young, and therefore not smart. Yet the problems we must face are not for the faint of heart. We are told to act like ladies and be quiet and polite. Next time you're told what to do, go and give them a fight." - Anonymous

Meditation: Think back to a time when you felt powerless. Minus self-criticism, re-experience it play by play. (Note that you're an observer, not a victim.) Now, using your imaginative power, recreate the story and *symbolically* take your power back. Maybe you imagine your power as a crystal, a light, your heart, etc. Place your hands on your navel and imagine the power being restored. Seal it with an "I will" affirmation (I will trust myself. I will stand up for me. I will speak against oppression in all forms. I will …).

LESSON 29

Recognizing Bad Vibes and Following Your Instincts

"You may not always know what's wrong, but I'll make damn sure you'll know when it ain't right." - Spirit speaking through Trelani Michelle (age 32 :: city 504)

Prompt: Think back to a time when it didn't feel right. You didn't know exactly what it was, but you know it wasn't right. What happened? Who was involved? How did you react? What was the result of that reaction?

Story: I think I was about sixteen when a friend invited me to tag along for a night out with some of her friends. When she asked, I agreed. As time grew closer to our evening out, I got a strong urge to stay home—not because my introverted preferences took over (which they're known to do), but because it just wasn't sitting right in my gut. While getting dressed, I felt so nauseous I thought I'd vomit. When she called to say they were on the way, tears welled up in my eyes. I couldn't explain the feeling, but I just knew that I had better not go. I now recognize what happened. My intuition was protecting me.

I don't always listen to my intuition. This is dangerous. I once went into an interview for a job that didn't feel right, got the job, and accepted it despite the bad vibes. Long story short, I was cornered in the back of a walk-in freezer and sexually assaulted. That's not to say that what happened was my fault, but it is to say that it could have possibly been avoided.

That feeling you just wrote about in your prompt? Mind it! Listen to it because you may not always know what's wrong, but Spirit will make damn sure you'll know when it ain't right.

"You must always be open in your spirit because, as women, our strength is the spiritual realm. You know we always feel things from our wombs." -Queen Afua, holistic practitioner and spiritual teacher

Meditation: Lie on your back and butterfly your legs, pressing the soles of your feet together (as comfortably as you can). Using your palms, gently press down on your womb and release. Go in rhythm with your breath as you pump life-energy into your sacral chakra.

LESSON 30

Walking in Your Truth

"Don't ever feel like someone who comes into your life is meant to stay there, and don't ever put more energy into someone than they put into you. Remember the entrance is always the exit." - Spirit speaking through Serenity (age 17 :: city 415)

Prompt:

1. Name one area of your life where you feel stuck.

2. List detailed options to get unstuck.

3. List your fears beginning with "What if."

4. List solutions to those fears.

5. Choose the option that feels best and create a scheduled to-do list for getting unstuck.

Story: My favorite and most memorable course in undergrad, by far, was Intro to Philosophy. It was the first class that required me to do such deep introspection, to put the textbook down and actually think about what I believed and why.

The professor asked the class what it would mean to us if we learned that God did not exist. "What would you do differently, if anything at all?" she asked. A huge part of me felt relieved that I wasn't the only one thinking this way. The last bit was a tad unnerved because, if there was no God, who would I pray to when shit went haywire? In summary, she proposed that the absence of an external deity pointed the finger back to us.

Your decision to read this book says that you've already embraced philosophy, and that you were ready to be a *knower* and no longer a believer. Being stuck is an option. Walk in that truth. *Know* your power and your responsibility in creating change and the life you wish to live. *Know* that you deserve it, and that everything you need to obtain it you either have already or haven't yet taken.

Meditation: Place your hands over your womb and say everything you want beginning with "I want." (I want to feel more beautiful. I want a car. I want to finish my book. I want …) Keep going until you're out of things to say.

LESSON 31

(Re)claiming Who You Be

"Don't be mad at yourself forever. Cry, take a nap, and feel better." -
Spirit speaking through **Kobe Duncan** (age 11 :: city 912)

Prompt: Make a list of fifty things you can do, within your means, to make yourself feel better.

Story: I tell my daughter all the time that you can't control what other people do and say. You can only control how you react to it. If your brother is getting on your nerves, leave the room. If your cousin made you cry, cry it out, but also decide how long you're going to let it keep you down. I think she inherited my godawful ability to take one upsetting moment and mull it over to the point that it ruins my entire day.

My friend Akilah S Richards shared something one day that changed my life. In the face of everything that's going on, ask yourself, "But how do I want to feel?" That question turns self-pity into self-responsibility. I woke up late, got a ticket on the way to class, the professor didn't even show up, and I dropped my phone and cracked my screen on the way back to my car. That's a bad ass day. I'ma sit in my car for about ten minutes, crying and cussing. Then I'm moving on, because I want to feel unbothered and at peace again. So I ask myself, "What can I do in this moment with what I have available to me right now to make myself feel unbothered and at peace again?" I'ma go to the lake, sit in my car with my seat reclined way back, and listen to my favorite playlist. Just like that, I've reclaimed my day.

Meditation: Let's put them all together, moving energy and power from your root to your crown. With all of these, keep going until you're out of things to say.

1. Sit on your hands and verbally express everything you are, beginning with "I am."

2. Place your hands on your womb and verbally express everything you want, beginning with "I want."

3. Place your hands over your navel and verbally express everything you will do/have, beginning with "I will."

4. Place your hands over your heart and verbally express everything you love, beginning with "I love."

5. Place your hands over your throat and verbally express everything you speak, beginning with "I speak."

6. Place your two fingers between your eyebrows and verbally express everything you foresee and see in the present, beginning with "I see."

7. Place your hands on the crown of your head and verbally express everything you know, beginning with "I know."

MERCI

We pray that this book resonated with you just as vividly as it did for us creating it. You can use it over and over again. As you know, we move in cycles. Growing, yeah, but also returning to the same lessons. That's what we wanted this book to be—one that you could return to and even share.

Creating sacred spaces to ask, answer, relate, heal, and grow is our responsibility. It's something we're extremely passionate about. We knew that it would take a special kind of girl to connect with the title *Girls Who Ain't Afraid to Curse When Communicating with God*, and you did. You are our tribe!

We're using the hashtags #GirlsWhoAintAfraid and #SpiritBeLike on social media, and invite you to use it for your own quotes from Spirit. This way, we can easily connect with one another.

We also have this podcast thing that we do, where we ask you a question and record your response to it. Before it's shared, though, you'll hear it first. That way, you can approve it or tell us to trash it. If you're interested in being a part of that, email Contact@SoFundamental.com.

"Me and you, us never part. Makidada. Me and you, us have one heart. Makidada. Ain't no ocean, ain't no sea. Makidada. Keep my sister away from me."

Sending you beaucoup love and light on your journey.

Warm regards,

Trelani and Jayla

ABOUT THE AUTHORS

I'm Jayla! An Aquarian who shares my private thoughts on public stages. I create poetry from things I learn throughout the day, but I stay inside most weekends. To revive my energy, I write some (and then some more) and keep in contact with my inner self.

I've been performing since the ninth grade, through The Deep Center and some of my own gigs. My work's touched stages from Tampa, Florida, to Las Vegas, Nevada; some of my poems have been featured in Savannah's Telfair Museum and the city's buses. Outside of my writing and performing, though, I make time to come back and reflect. On my own actions, how I could improve, or if I let enough of my true, unfiltered self come out rather than society's "acceptable" version.

Now that I've grown and graduated or whatever, I finally feel ready. To find poetry in conversation and healing in vulnerability, and to add to the never-ending stories of self-expression.

--

And I'm Trelani :) My name means Three Heavens, and people tend to think of me as an Erykah Badu type chick, whatever that means (although I know exactly what that means). Could be a Pisces thing. I don't take offense and I agree to an extent. But everybody eyebrows go up at some point in unraveling me.

What shocks them is usually learning that I've written A LOT of books—even some for famous folk—that I sat next to Nikki Giovanni once during lunch, and that I raise a fifteen- and eleven-year-old, and theyon't have a bedtime. I graduated from SSU and SCAD but still think college is overpriced and sometimes overrated, started working at fourteen (twelve if you count being the candygirl at school), worked my way to the Library of Congress, and then re-realized I'm way more passionate about projects like *Krak Teet* and *Girls Who Ain't Afraid*.